It is good to be alive—and to be counted among the humans. This is how I have felt every time I have seen To Be Alive! *There is insecurity, anxiety and fear aplenty in our world. But there is also goodness and the sheer joy of living all around us. And there can be understanding amongst us. This is why all of us—and the United Nations as well—can hope for and can foresee a future for mankind.*

Ralph J. Bunche

UNITED NATIONS

to be alive!

From the Film Produced
by Francis Thompson, Inc.
for Johnson Wax

Text by Alastair Reid

BOOK DESIGN BY THEODORE KAMECKE

The Macmillan Company, New York
Collier-Macmillan Limited, London

The theme and pictures for this book
are taken directly from the film, *To Be
Alive!*, commissioned by S. C. Johnson
& Son, Inc. of Racine, Wisconsin, and
exhibited at their New York World's
Fair Pavilion in 1964-1965. *To Be Alive!*
was filmed on location in Africa, Europe
and the United States. Following are
acknowledgments to those who worked
on it:

Directed by:	Francis Thompson
	Alexander Hammid
Production Staff:	Peter Robinson
	Peter Powell
	Theodore Kamecke
	Richard Adams
	Richard Forstmann
	Joan Piker
Film Narration	
Written by:	Edward Field
Spoken by:	Robert Fields
Music:	Gene Forrell

Dedicated to Herbert F. Johnson

Library of Congress Catalog Card
Number: 66-29052

The Macmillan Company, New York
Collier-Macmillan Canada, Ltd., Toronto

Lithography by Barnes Press, Inc.
PRINTED IN THE UNITED STATES OF AMERICA

FIRST PRINTING

Introduction

When S. C. Johnson and Son, Inc. asked us to make a film to be shown in their Pavilion at the New York World's Fair of 1964-1965, their proposal sounded like a film-maker's dream: Make a motion picture any way you like as long as it is entertaining, does not exceed eighteen minutes and expresses the Fair's theme, "Peace Through Understanding." Producing a film is an expensive enterprise and film-makers are rarely given such an opportunity. We were both elated by our good fortune and troubled lest we fail to take full advantage of it. Should a film devoted to "Peace Through Understanding" try to approach head-on such obvious and painful stumbling-blocks as war, overpopulation, and the rise of nationalism? Questions of artistry aside, how effective would this approach seem to audiences coming to the Fair in a holiday mood, quite naturally unprepared to think hard, bleak thoughts? We sensed that it would be bad tactics as well as bad art simply to lecture our audiences. We hoped to convey our thoughts by touching their emotions rather than simply resting on logic.

In the end, we found that we had several goals we wished to achieve. We would hope to leave our audiences convinced that, despite the pessimism with which the world faces an ever-increasing burden of problems, man is not a lost cause—is not even a losing cause. We would hope to show that, though misery and suffering are widespread, it is possible for people to live happy and fruitful lives. We would hope to show that the number of people who lead such lives can and must be increased, and we would hope to indicate that this increase can come about because people have more in common than they suppose—because we are all more alike than the variety of our colors and physiognomies and curious local customs would imply, and these likenesses have only to be imaginatively grasped and made use of to transform our relations with each other. We decided that the best way to demonstrate the existence of these possibilities was to depict the amount of joyous life that is experienced from day to day all round the world, so often modestly and unexceptionally that one scarcely bothers to notice it. In depicting this we would be suggesting that there is no need either to despair of the turbulent present or to long for some sleek, highly automated future, in which many of our contemporary human problems would have been resolved by the abolition of our humanity.

Perhaps the film and this book don't state as much as is stated here. Still, it is what we believe and it is what we intended to convey. It only remains to add that the degree to which we have succeeded is thanks to the understanding and hard work of every member of the group who worked with us in making *To Be Alive!*

Francis Thompson

To pull the blinds of habit from the eyes,
to see the world without names for the first bright time,
to wander through its mystery, to wonder
at every age and stage, at one with it—
to be alive!

day in day out day in day out next please next please yes no stop go no turn in out up down watch your step next please

seventeen eighteen twentythree fifty seven
what was the number time to get ready
now where did I put now where I forget
and what was the where is the yes no next
forty-one

I remember tomorrow too late . . .

next please   next please   next please   yes no   yes no   next please   clickety-click   stop go   clickety-click

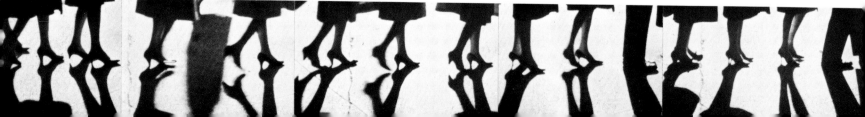

push pull   clickety-click   press turn   clickety-click   quick quick quick quick tick tick tick tick . . . WAIT!

I read new lessons in the leaves
I breathe with the wind in the flickering grass
I tell my time by the teetering tortoise
Slowly I open my ears and my eyes

And then I begin to move, faster and faster, giving the world a whirl, spinning into tomorrow . . .

I'm going to ride my faithful steed all across Africa doing great deeds and everyone will like me and make me king . . .

I'm going to sail my boat all the way to America and discover it over again . . .

And, as I swing into the sky
I feel I am flying into a future.

All I once knew
falls away under me.
There is wind in my head.
How high are clouds?
Will I ever come down?
The sky holds its breath.

Each day is a beginning.
Each day I am new.

Sometimes I solve the secrets in spiderwebs,
follow lost paths into the depths of the forest,
listen to animals talking together,
and laugh at the centipede humping home.
Just gazing, I grow small enough to sit on a twig.
I can be any size I want to be . . .

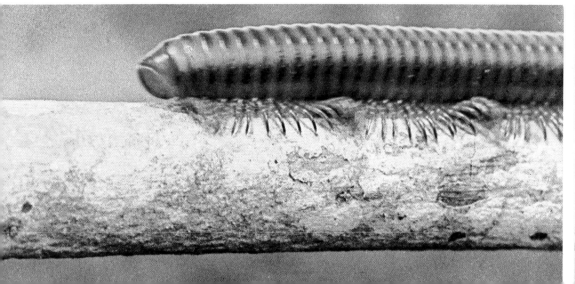

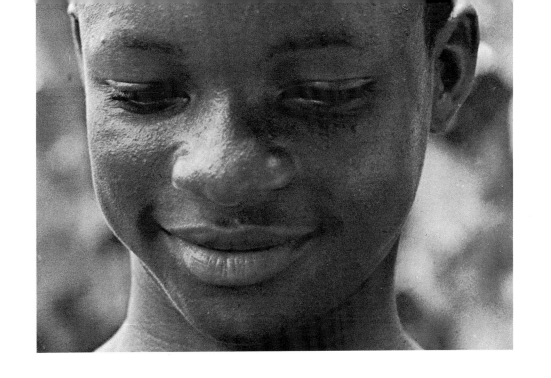

Sometimes I transform the world.
I take my glass prism
and hold it up to my eyes.

Everything dances with color
as I turn the glass in my hand.
The city becomes a rainbow,
the buildings shimmer with light.

Do you ever feel joy grow like a bubble
bigger and bigger inside you?
When I do, it makes me want to call
good news to the whole town . . .

run wild through the streets
knocking on doors
climbing on rooftops
higher and higher

till I reach the stairs
that lead to the tower
at the top of the town . . .

I pull the rope
and the bubbles burst
and go rolling rolling
in a jangle of bells
telling my joy
all over the town and away . . .

When the wind gets into us, we go off, flying, flying . . .
wheels unrolling the roads before us, wild with speed . . .

On on on . . .

Will we ever reach that point where the road touches the sky?

There is no point.
There is only moving.
We leave our selves behind.
Our wheels unwind us.

What will we find at the end?
Our selves again, but changed.

Crash! and, winded, we come back to earth,
full of dust and laughter, wiser than we were.

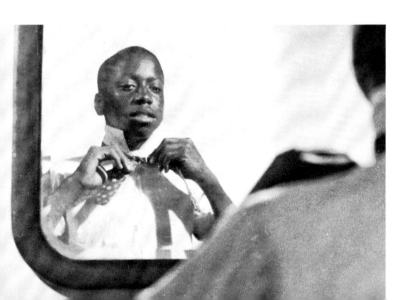

What do you do with your hair when it won't go where you want it?

Which face will I wear today? Who shall I be?

Will I ever get to know the stranger in the mirror?

But when we are out in the world,
there is no time to wonder,
no time to breathe,
so much is happening.
The time goes singing away . . .

Our heroes are taking our breath away.
Will one of them swoop down from the clouds
and carry us off?

Mornings on the water
with the river singing.
Girls with their eyes alight,
boys twirling their paddles.
We glide on our own laughter.
We float on our own delight.

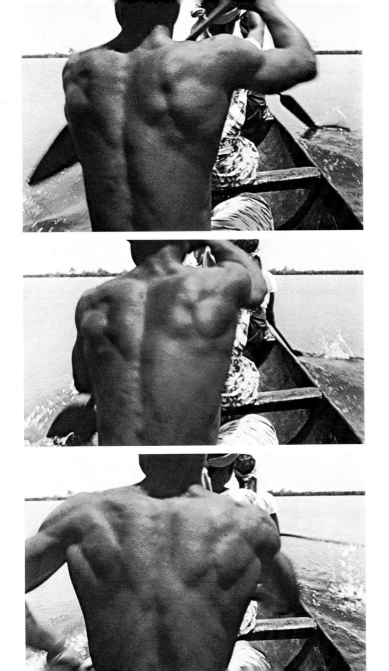

Take my hand. Take my hand.
There is something still to understand.

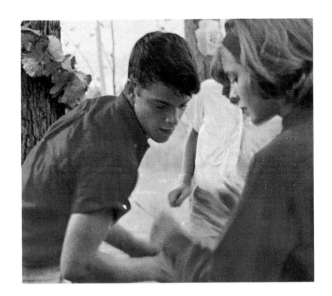

There are lessons to learn our books never taught.
There are things our parents forgot.

If I could tell you what can never be said.
Listen. I have birds in my head,
stars in my feet, clouds on my mind.

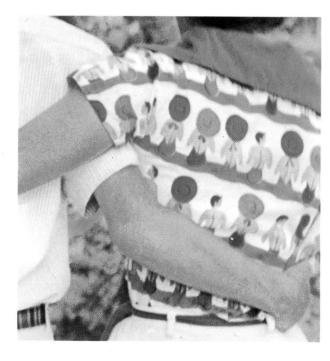

So try to understand.
Take my hand.

Then, suddenly, two by two,
we turn
a new surprising corner . . .

It was a new kind of seeing,
a new kind of knowing.

Warily, warily
we met, talked, touched,
and from the silence of aloneness,
we moved together.

We regretted the end of every moment.
Could it not always be like this?
Don't let it slip away.
Grasp it, hold it, make it stay.

Will you promise? I promise.
Forever? For ever.

So we took our vows,
and on the day of our wedding . . .

there was more wine than glasses, more food than plates, more feet than shoes, more kisses than lips . . .

something was ending,
something was beginning.

The days open their arms, and we go out to the fields, or down to the sea
to harvest the ripe fruits of the morning . . .

out of the slow processes of the earth and the turbulent rumble of great cities,

out of the crossing of past and future, out of great continents of difference . . .

the vaults of the past tower over us,
and, walking in their shadow,
in awe, we turn to face
the empty space of the future . . .

we hold the present in our hands,
hands that put together new shapes,

that gather the fruits of the turning seasons . . .

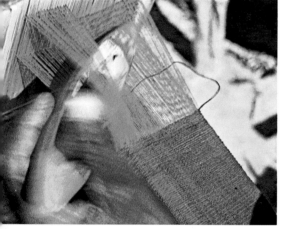

hands that are weaving primal patterns,

that give to things a human shape . . .

hands that grope for forms in clay,

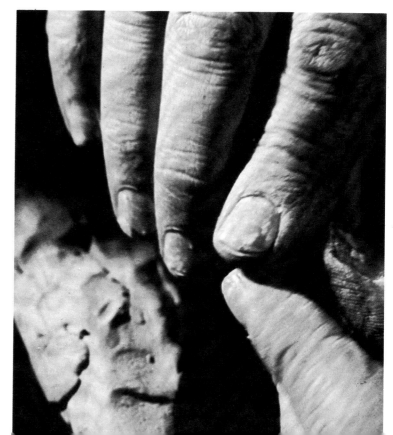

and grace the forms of everyday . . .

hands that play with the color of feeling
in rooms of the mind, on a silent canvas.

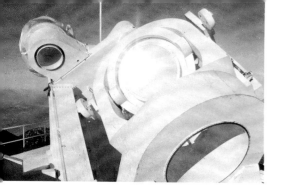

We bring the sun, from the distances of space,
down to our table. We turn it over
in wonder—energy, warmth, light—
like a great gold coin, an unattainable treasure.
It rings true. But it is not ours to keep.
Observed, respected, it is the source of mystery,
as once it was the source of fear.
Now, we have shed the fear and retain the wonder.
Slowly the unknown, under our questioning eyes,
yields up its secrets and reveals
new shapes, new worlds, new possibilities.
We go out, like children, into the vastness of space
and bring back news. The sun shimmers
in the sky, in the telescope. The patient watchers
gaze into space, waiting, wondering . . .

And once in a while, we take
a day out of time, to meet, to celebrate
the world which made us and which we are making . . .

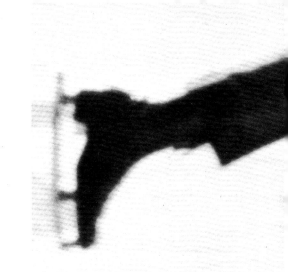

helping each other to find our feet.
Take my hand. Take my hand.

Does the water go on a long way?
Yes, boy, further than you or I can imagine.
Is the water old then?
Neither old nor young. It just goes on.
Will I be as old as you are? Will I be as old as that frog?
What is it like to be old?
It is all just floating on the water, on and on.

Grandfather what is this?
It is called milkweed, boy. Let it fly.
Look, it goes up and up. Is it alive?
Yes, in its way. Can you still see it?
It's higher than the birds. I've lost it now. I wish
I could fly.

You will, boy, in your way.

Grandfather, tell me about flying.
Tell me about water. Tell me about everything.
Tell me what it is, to be alive.

To Be Alive! *was made for projection onto three
separate screens set side by side and curving slightly
around the audience. Most scenes were photographed
with three synchronized cameras, producing a single
continuous image. For both technical and esthetic
reasons narrow gaps were left between the screens.
Viewers were surprised to find that the gaps
disappeared in the mind when a single, continuous
image filled the three screens, and conversely when
three different images were projected simultaneously,
the gaps emphasized their separateness. This film
technique gave us a novel means of expression: we
could, at will, unify, break up, contrast, juxtapose or
compare various images while maintaining a
continuous esthetic whole on the three screens.*

*The pictures in this book were taken directly from the
film. The layout of the pages of course follows the
graphic requirements of a book, and thus it departs
somewhat from the sequence and arrangement of
images as they appeared in the film. Nevertheless, the
three-screen technique as described above is reflected
in the book by the white lines which divide some of
the pictures in much the same way as the gaps
divided the theatre screens.*

70
71
72
74
75
76
77
79
83
85